Animal Chat

series ©

Jeffsgaff Studio Productions presents

Best Friends are Always Bald

by Jeff Ree

This book belongs to

_____

Book #2 from the "Animal Chat" series
created and published by
Jeffsgaff Entertainment & Studio Productions
Limerick, Ireland

for more information, go to books.jeffsgaff.ie

Shawn tells his dogs
their coats need a clean

Shampoo and a cut,
but what can that mean?

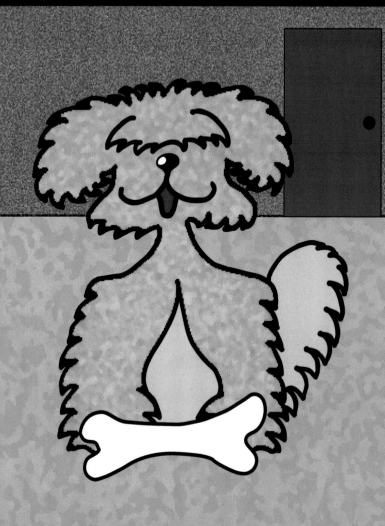

This one is Star
and that one's Murray

Their hairy heads
are full of worry

Star is so vain,
he thinks he is great

He wants to be sure
to tell his mate

They bark and growl
and bark some more

Until Shawn takes Star
to the room next door

BUZZ

BUZZ

BUZZ

Star can be heard by
his howl and his bark

HOWL
BARK

As the razor shaves away his fur in the dark

17

BUZZ

BUZZ

BUZZ

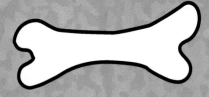

The buzzing sends Murray
to sleep on the floor

Until Shawn walks in
and slams the door

19

He chops and he shaves
the furry old mutt

Both dogs are not like
they were before

With their furry coats
cast off on the floor

Murray is cold
and far from happy

But then he sees
a brand new chappy

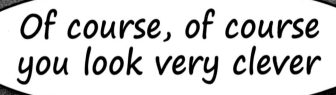

The
End

"Thank you for reading 'Best Friends Are Always Bald.' I hope you learn from Star and Murray that everyone can be friends despite their differences. Please share this book with all your friends"

– Jeff Ree